GOOD GAME

Andrew K. Peterson

SPUYTEN DUYVIL
NEW YORK CITY

Gratitude to the fearless editors of the small press journals where some of these poems lived: The Ekphrastic Review, Mass Poetry, Moss Trill, No Infinite Issue 4 Election Special, Oddball Magazine, Other Rooms Press' Open Resistance Issue, Otoliths, Reality Beach, Truck, and What Rough Beast. Also, great cheers to the small press publishers who supported these poems in various chapbooks: *The Big Game Is Every Night*, published by William Allegrezza at Moria/Locofo Chaps; *Doom Brunch*, published by Kent Johnson and Michael Boughn at Dispatches from the Poetry Wars; *Other Delights*, published by Susana Gardner and Elisabeth Workman at Dusie; *Brighton Nights*, published by CC Hannett as a Disappearing Chapbook at Really Serious Literature; and *and so, a vineyard*, published by rob mclennan at above/ground press. Also, big game ups to Tod Thilleman and Aurelia at Spuyten Duyvil for making this book sing.

Much thanks and love to my family, and especially to Michele Lubowsky, for your unerring support, patience, understanding, and grace. Much love to my poetry gang, art community, and friends who I cannot do without: Tim Armentrout, Reed Bye, Amina Cain, Joseph Cooper, Jim Dunn, Cynthia Schwartzberg Edlow, Bridget Eileen, Soma Feldmar, Lark Fox, Susana Gardner, Elizabeth Guthrie, jj hastain, Jared Hayes, HR Hegnauer, Ben Hersey, Kevin Kilroy, Jonah Kinchy, Michael Koshkin, Travis & JenMarie Macdonald, Audrey Mardavich, Suzanne Mercury, John Mulrooney, Tanya Phattyakul, Mike Puretz, Jennifer Rogers, Bob Roley, John Sakkis, Kate Jean Spencer, Celeste Davis Stragand, Charlotte Seley, August Smith, Luis Humberto Valadez, Donald Vincent, Danielle Vogel, Rainey Warren, Jane Werle, and Andrew Wessels. Also, cheers to the folks who organized events and readings where some of this work was presented, including Christina Davis at Harvard University's Woodberry Poetry Room; Jessica Bozek at Small Animal Project; Bridget Eileen and Suzanne Mercury at Boston Poetry Marathon; and Mitch Manning at No Infinite. Good game, all.

Good Game
© 2020 Andrew K. Peterson
ISBN 978-1-949966-92-3

Published by Spuyten Duyvil Publishing
spuytenduyvil.net
All Rights Reserved.

Front Cover Art by Andrew K. Peterson
Book Layout by T. Thilleman

Author Photo by Joseph Cooper

Library of Congress Cataloging-in-Publication Data

Names: Peterson, Andrew K., author.
Title: Good game / Andrew K. Peterson.
Description: New York City : Spuyten Duyvil, [2020] |
Identifiers: LCCN 2020004607 | ISBN 9781949966923 (paperback)
Subjects: LCGFT: Poetry.
Classification: LCC PS3616.E84272 G66 2020 | DDC 811/.6--dc23
LC record available at https://lccn.loc.gov/2020004607

Contents

THE BIG GAME IS EVERY NIGHT
The Big Game is Every Night / 1
Poem on Joan Mitchell's Birthday / 2
Polar Bear and Rosé / 3
Doom Brunch / 4
Blossom Feedback / 6
Born at Night / 7
If It's Not Love Then It's The Bomb The Bomb The Bomb That Will
    Keep Us Together / 9
Sad Clown Portrait / 11
Better Waterfalls / 13
Serious Moonlight / 14
Arsonist's Daughter / 15
Cluster Glitters / 16
Never Be Royals / 17
Revelation / 18
Gold in Skeleton / 19
Notes for Beast Narration / 20

GOOD GAME
Call Script / 25
Poem for Nasty Women / 26
Poem Placed on the Green Monster During Law Enforcement
    Counterterror Practice Fenway Park June 12th 2016 / 28
Poem to be Dropped into Encore Boston Harbor Resort and Casino
    Construction Site July 2019 (Failed) / 30
Poem Placed on BU Footbridge Over Storrow Drive Where Santos
    Laboy was Shot and Killed by Massachusetts State Trooper
    June 19th 2015 / 32
Poem Placed in an Old Pair of New Balance Sneakers and Left on
    New Balance Factory Outlet Store Stoop on Berrigan's
    Birthday November 15 2016 / 33
Poem to be Read Aloud on the Corner of Massachusetts Ave. and
    Newbury St. on International Worker's Day / 34

Poem for The Earth Archive / 36
Poem for Empire / 38
Poem for a Disappearing Roommate / 41
Poem for Alice Coltrane on International Women's Day / 43
Sycamore Flesh / 44

PHILIP WHALEN SITTING ZAZEN
Amida / 49
Sunshine Umbrella / 50
My Heart Is Full of Buffalo Wings / 51
Love Parade / 52
Auld Lang Signifier / 53
The Great Midwestern Hardware Store / 54
Poem for Businessmen or, Wrong Shirt / 55
Begging Bowl / 56
Philip Whalen Sitting Zazen / 57

BRIGHTON NIGHT / 59

DESIRE LINE
Desire Line / 73
Blue Acrobat / 74
High Contrast / 76
Some Pleasant Moments in the Twenty-First Century / 80
Everybody is a Star / 86
weather, not ocean / 87
R.E.M. Suite / 90
Dear Reed Bye, / 93
An autumnal / 94
Water Lilies / 95
Other Delights / 96
Elegy with Saffron & Honey / 97
Two Sherpas / 99
The Beginning / 100

Notes / 103

simplicity stands at the end, not at the beginning
Anni Albers

The Big Game is Every Night

The Big Game Is Every Night
i.m. Jason Molina

being young enough to know *enough*
& maybe not keep reburning
the Civil War? should i give up on
giving into disbelief? maybe stop
letting chains binge on charms of
my lover's mouth?

in a pink pink pink punk swoon
love adjusts its difficulties,
readjusts power as you can
make a mirror warm & fall back
into love of one more thing
as vulnerable clarity

through their going
some return to you
the impact of needing,
kneaded through alms
that steady the blush,
skim the lake for good vibrations

small and unhidden –
slow going, but it *is* going

it's a big game
& the big game is every night
a mountainous rose
swells of diamond surfers,
dub sparks on the moon's hood,
a wolf at the brim of her kind

Poem on Joan Mitchell's Birthday

I could wake as if you weren't already
here   the light from my mouth to your
eyes   the light from my eyes to your
mouth all set to flourish, stranger,
touch my shoulder with your glove

with as much parking as you can muster
I love this part of New York
I don't live in – your coat
on slow and volatile
takes me home into the fading

snap-cold cold snap
carries its moon in a pail of blue hair
belief me grief me beyond these walls of kale-
reminiscent sweetness
reaching out to anger
asks for what it wants

which is nothing,
wild blueberry
when I could
in the middle of that blued & purple cinema
the bandaid's gone

form shatters the void
as a knife   slides off her palette

Polar Bear and Rosé

Say when   when
in the kingdom of enough is enough is enough
is enough   Say when   when
Your favorite utopias lie unlisted among
hypercolor presents & baked Freon pools
from the city's many working window units   when
what I cannot stir is what I cannot ask   when
so what I don't know is what to say   when
I have to say something to hurl myself at the hill
that scores everything unsummoned
in a symphony for the school district's
thousand broken instruments
with a bowed bass-line
at the bottom of its vibrating wheel
Let it be the cloud above, a leveler
Above my tiny kingdom of buttercups   say when
When you say say when and I say when   when
we both just about fill to the brim
                            without going over, then

Doom Brunch
for Jared Hayes

"Myth? Ray, has it ever occurred to you that the reason we've been so busy
lately is because the dead *have* been rising from the grave?"
"How about a little music?" – Ghostbusters

my endless feed a hungry ghost
a friend says Jung says "it is indeed possible
imagine our own death" folding into mall-walkers
seamless without notice by the shuttered Orange Julius
when 1999 was soooo 1984 in 1983
like we don't know we're immortal as any other motherfucker out here
The riders still riding, the raiders still raiding.
The lovers' hearts' still.
The let-me-put-my-beers-in-this-box-hey-fellas-wait-up-I-brought-this-box-
I-think-it-would-be-good-to-carry-some-beers-in kinda guys
Still doing a thing as they climb the roof to watch the sky remove itself
against each other upright to retreat from
the pressure of stacking one on top of the other.
We are a hospitable species, though to a fault;
last night I dreamed you to a doom brunch:
The city quiet street for a momentary etude when
"nothing has recently found to be forever"
if some friends forget the evite maybe another remembers
Hey-guys-give-me-a-hand-with-this-box-we-can-carry-some-beers-in-to-
gether-guys?-nothing-has-recently-found-to-be-forever
The end of the world doesn't matter, this box
Doesn't matter. The poem in the other room
about making it to leave work early get a little time
burn one down the last embers the splatter rise above
rooftops baring steaming summer teeth, little
disappointments and daring plights of city talk's flights and
burdens inherited and learned, the inconsistencies
loose beers in a box rattling
smoke of this ceremonial emoji incense stick

with a thought for the dear departed lady
The riders still riding, the raiders still raiding.
The lovers' hearts' still
flags   how about a little music?
Over the bridge we go – a red right night
beats to the ache of this electrolytic longing

Blossom Feedback

burnt orange
dry husk
redemption centers
in relation to crisp gala
guests a cross between
frank & scarlet (as if!
land a difference
toss a few stiff gardenias
back into the mix &
tomorrow we'll sting
peeling off the vine-
heavy tangle sheer
silhouette – morning's
blossom feedback –
what rind remembers
redeems them
ancient parchments
because tonight
tomorrow belongs
to dried orchids
the exiled slung
through fog to the
capitol, pistils in air

Born at Night

I love you so much fun
in the I-can't-stand-it
sullen dulls and trellises
born at night
when I have to be good
to be a good time
The fact is I can't see it's fact

I can't tell the difference:
The only thing that it could have and
The only thing that I should have
I can see it as excuse
I love for its necessity
& let it back in

when the fact is to live
when you're at a time
what you need to
to have a good night
be a new version
of the same old ways
to love is to have

some living proof
no one said it's an easy
on the edge of that dark lake
on my way home to work
the best part of the day
when I get to be good
for strangers on the bus

in my mind & leave them
I love you so much fun
I know you mean to love me too
after a squall crossing
border leaves
so much fun
the quaint way

a quiet man stomps
snow & salts the quiet
in the middle of a squall
a calm New England way
a living proof
will I inherit? quiet?
in the middle of a squall

If It's Not Love Then It's The Bomb The Bomb The Bomb That Will Keep Us Together

The wall with a door is something I had to have. – Georgia O'Keefe

Things to do in the din: slip
away, fall off, balk back double
time. Turn down the bridge

reverb in a robin's egg. Cop
a whisper. The universe is
smaller in America. Scream.

Walk the driest latitudes crushing on
bustling pink flowers of a burnt gown
grown wide with bark-fried tears. Radiate

gaucho dusk. Wander out from blunderings,
back to the street, empties in pockets,
practice late capitalism with minimalist pan-

ache: huddle vulnerable with soft
secrets at the ATM brushed smooth
by smooth jazz pouring down the crack

of a lion's ass. Seek loss in false stops
or risks too loose. What's nobler?
Trust that lowers, lilacs. Also, memory.

You're the water in a congress
of the best thing I can do
today: get money off my mind.

This isn't fate, it's just what's to get.
Really, who put the bomb in the bomb
sh'bomb. Bloop. Still tested over the sea.

A willow-spun joke, a fathom's
dumb depths. Tightly wished at.
cusps   Crush out. Shimmer.

Rest the rest in morning air's
illusions simmered into.
Summon in summer faster.

Sad Clown Portrait

would've hexed late discomforts
with mossy voladeros
but for morning's thorn-trumpets'
preemptive counter-hex

would've ooh childed insomnia
with a minotaur orchid
but for my sad rosed talisman
couldn't let go of the fire

would've supplanted anxious chance
with indecent taste
but for dark raid sprays
from somnambulant third eyes

would've challenged the infinite
to dueling banjos
but for digitalis intimations'
grave amateur hour status

would've canted orbit's milligrams
with augmenting fates
but for martinis of fire
propping up my yuppie front

would've asked for all your love
I would I would've
but for the demon me believed
I couldn't keep up

would've given up on all the rest
but for sky's living museum
running on fumes
blithe river gowns

gathering the rests
for all the grace of your unknowns

BETTER WATERFALLS
for Joe Bender

some of the better
waterfalls have lead
times of several
hundred thousand
years! a wound rivers
until an ever riven-
venom of movers
mend a miramar or
stand a pyramid
on its head, not worry
as it topples, ringing
how rebellion governs
in a demonstrating
negative absolute
you don't need to tell
the better water
fallers: it's time
to fall, not worry
as it topples, ringing
out, it's only now,
and only just arriving

Serious Moonlight
i.m. David Bowie

moonlight   a monument to memory's fresh dance clothes set to tremble
moonlight   the road's laminate foxglove blotting out forgottens –
moonlight   on a violin eyelashéd dilated lunar synthesizer
moonlight   whales swimming backwards to the top of a waterfall
moonlight   windows in a bubble ~ afternoon plain-sight
moonlight   faster than sap
moonlight   above a genocide, would you moonlight if you knew?
moonlight   on a crowd of blue-haloed mourners
moonlight   pained minerals on the orphan chapel ceiling
moonlight   above friends' arms linked in protest
moonlight   from all directions where you cannot reach
moonlight   ghost conch ululating alms culminating in urn-flame
moonlight   on the moon where neither seem lost
moonlight   in the moonlight
                         in the serious moonlight
                                           oh, unserious moon

Arsonist's Daughter
i.m. Bobbie Louise Hawkins

A bald cypress, the lone witness: "If it weren't for Madeline,
grown and gone snorting moonlight's paragon grooves

mending hems of midnight suns some Oslo summer,
we wouldn't have much to argue," sips rainwater in windturn.

"She is not the daughter, it continues," dipping its roots.
"The father is a graceless dolt, timid, and harmless.

She is not the daughter; not sad laughter. Sparse remnants,
dune memory. A resonance of touch the neighborhood mourns.

She is flames, flames on the side of my face heavingbreathless
heaving breaths. She is the arsonist." Past ash's limit, breaks

From the honeybunch tangerine trench to this taut limpid limn.
Past as far as she can go, she does go.

Heavingbreathless.
Is limitless and conjuring.

Cluster Glitters
i.m. Jack Collom

you know, he said, you have a real talent for dreams
I had hoped, of course that the world would stand still

how many violins does it really take to wave goodbye?
how they dive and drive by night to the fix of their resolve
to still the whirl and flay of the glitter clusters

& though the ambers make me limber
cut from the edge of vanity
shatter out tired schemes
rawer nerve gone steadily on,
sweetening the splay,
the complexities of oh...
in deference to lack i have forgotten
    hibiscus,
      raspberry

falls in among pale lumbering
bud-iced ringlets,
the violet phenomenal hinge
opens onto 9 or 10 likes
equal to two weeks' ago blue

kind, unexpected early thunder-snow
wrinkles yesterday's pink blossoms

Never Be Royals
for Charlotte Seley

The road from Providence is lit with many perils
Bouncing oceans burn from new moons
Old stars mix with snow and indiscreet
Leaning, faulty debutante flair, pale and fault-
Less loose roost and more abandoned rope
Of the snake lady, her diamonds bright fires
In marshmallow clover   bustling fancy
Free among trifles   reefs   glistening
Riffs Lou Reed Stole   i.e. The Black Angel's Death Song's
From Getz and Gilberto's   Vivo Sohando
Countering faults with offerings
The road to Providence is lit with petty morals
At the limit   this too timid limb
Priestess who knows
No compromise, the skull and rose are
Equals, line august roads along these low low lands

Revelation

I had a thought that I could change – Doug + Jean Carn

Okay here comes grief
winter, the metaphor,
fails, egg-hued
mulberry and brown

Winter, the distant bodied
wolf's claw blue
displaced, fails

& did feel regret, did burn
sweetgrass, salt sage
As an asking

The birch shell upfalling
through cloud-sheaths
welled upon the rainblown sea

Cutting through attachments
a whirlwind's impossible hymn –

The silence inside
is named   Unfolds
from a wreathed galaxy
poppied to the take :

a touch-chosen
          laughing
                kelp ring
in the teeth of a rose-bladed rudder

Gold in Skeleton

chord orchid's
lone skid
in orchard cherried
suffers of thought –

        o curl
            my yurt for
                a honeycomb
     intuit –

a force devours
meat of cold rain
struggles, a rippled-
out lightning twist

        along the mystic
        6/8 time   steeps
        what i forget
        moves the sun

above your hospice
gives through
snow's skylight melt
its grace, grace

        i thank to know
        thank the thanks
        the goodbyes
        the have-been-knowns

Notes for Beast Narration
for Tim Armentrout

Hey pink cloud,
unmask me
Hey roommate at dawn
pick me off the floor
with your eyelash lagoon,
stardust banter, backwards eloquence.
Hey beast spirit,

Let me climb onto your comb.
let your rain down
on magnolia whispers
with how heights speak
confessions
what leaves whisper,
fumbles out the towers'

gold-leafed light rims
tipped with parapets of loss
How we are veterans of lust
pinned equalizers
bent torture and disorder
the war with no whole,
the warp with no keeper

I hold on your green, hold
to the shunt of your coast
with my algaes of need
soft as feathered Nike
breached by scorpions
   twisted within dams'
hippie jade & desert sunset

vans, cadillacs of dawn-
feather by feather
stripped wonder
molt a mauve puce
a punk lean against the hood
heathered by feather we flow
heathered by feather we flow

heathered by feather we
heather
the breathing curtains' wheel-maw
hey ember of an untethered hum
hey
let me comb and be lost
among hills of rhombic might

pushing up a pyramid kiss
against a morning cloud
against a gnashing gobbled class
singed & singing back
against the roaring

Good Game

Call Script

Hello Senator, piercing and apportioned
Below the lazing drones we summer
In the consequence of keeping
Full charge with the real Reality
Winner. Senator, dinosaurs are somewhere
Rooting for us, – the fables of Faubus,
Foibles of gooble gobble –
Bird-ghost bodies & bone maps,
Some pleasanter moments in the century of
CSPAN community access.
No one's in charge, the situation's
The boss. If you do not ring the bell and
No one's on the platform this economy
Can't stop won't stop. Theeese yeses, aaaare crying,
These yeses have seen a lot of loves but
They're never gonna see another one like I
Had with you, Senator. Only love's infinite
Divisions and finite indivisibles remain, a minor
Limit in ancient imitation of democracy. If only
I could live off the ice cream money,
Safe and insured, unshaven and couth.
Theeese yeses, I shall not wait to hang upon
The count of your crook and starry vote
But raise the black flag, and burn in white,
Unplug me but from rainbow watts and nettles,
Bank balance on sea snails to lay their eggs in moonlight
Unsheathe this trusty conch and uncork its wild pitches
Signal a flask of mermaid senators to swim ruggedly ashore

Text of voicemail messages left on the Washington office voicemails of Republican Senators Susan Collins, Dean Heller, and Rand Paul in advance of Affordable Health Care Appeal vote while standing at the edge of Cambridge's Annual Citywide Dance Party on June 30, 2017.

Poem for Nasty Women

Reading Eileen but without
the confidence. angst
is a cave, dank &
plain, drawn in
rest on the flight
out to Egypt. No,
Nantasket Beach,
in a Mercury, from
Minerva to Aglauros:
bake me out of this stone.
I sleep in your spirit
blued shadow mouth
with three white tulips

lightning bolts
against an iceberg.
The guard guarding
protecting & protected
by beauty all day
looks stoned
"simplicity
defies resolution"

How's it any moment
I'm repping denim, flannel,
leather, rubber, fleece,
alpaca, yak's wool
copper orangutan
college sweatshirt

"step out of your comforts of illusion"
into samsaric armfuls
less than and far from these removals
as I hoped

I wouldn't be
losing you Eileen
losing this
fantasy game
the driver whipping
around an MFA drop off circle
avoiding waddlers
gaggling the fens
express this
blinding lack of reciprocity
as Staties ha-
ranguing that hydrant blocker

Reading Eileen
without the confidence
makes curl & sway
a deer in arrow-light
foam cups
an aching cloud
so the flag snaps
backwards
the tune of
my illusions
this time
leading with stars

Poem Placed on the Green Monster During Law Enforcement Counterterror Practice Fenway Park June 12th 2016

Unarmed & unarmed
awake awake awake
we dance
that peace we dance
that space of

peace, a list of wildflowers
catalogued a century of Junes
ago returns to undo your removals,
silence tacks of the hammers,
the spells of summer in our eyes

   Castanea, Borage, Buxus, Rubus,
  Campanula pyramidalis,
  Aquileiga, Cupressus,
  Bellis simplex Bellis perennis,
  Arum dracunculus, Fritillaria imerialis,

  Narcissus Sylvestris,
  Digitalis, Erica vulgaris,
 Iris flammea, Arundo bambos,
   Xaranthemum anunm, Junipurnis,
  Lilium, Asphodelus

Unarmed and unarmed
& ache, & ache, & ache
we dance that space
we dance that peaced out
space overheats the wax from your wings

to the sun-high priestess of flower bullets
oh complex city heart
with baked out prudence
let spells of summer transmit from thine eyes

Poem to be Dropped into Encore Boston Harbor Resort and Casino Construction Site Everett MA July 2019 (Failed)

Blood summons the diamond-
harbor city wakes that long for
net-lit passage, smoked copper
dome mouth pouring sage-lipped
incense nailed to concrete.

Harbor the city in wakes
that long for disgrace
smuggled blue unions
elephant labrum, moss,
labor's musk. Continuation's

Busked out grace rents years
in a tilt among climates for a sphinx
eye to fill. Snow melts the pyramids
releasing bones of tyrants, peaceful kings,
forgotten golds from a rift orchard.

Share these abandoned names
with the storm that brings erosion
in ragtime-braced floods, headless
birds, free stuff & lost hoodies.
Beneath torrents: violet skies,

Deranged rovers beneath cap space,
beneath tea-flooded tides. Vacuums
the leopard from domesticate wheel
fire, frailing and framming. Wash
Atlantic Rivieras out with foam

Ash, lost deliveries, dismantled search
engines. Blossom and return
illusions on reckless city rewind.
Blossom, oi urchin pattern
fire-netted floors, resistant forests.

Blossom and anew, release.

Poem Placed on BU Footbridge Over Storrow Drive Where Santos Laboy Was Shot and Killed by Massachusetts State Trooper June 19th 2015

Thorn-trees bloom
by a little village
in southern Brazil
named, I'm told,
misunderstanding
a loose translation,
for nearby thorns —

Não-Me-Toque —
(Don't-Touch-Me)
will not cross
you anymore,
bridge crossed too many times

when I can barely hold my own
hands, it forgives;
when there's nothing to —
forget it. Forgive me
all my words — touch
is a form of absence.

Não-Me-Toque.
Não-Me-Toque.

No need to chase a man
just because he runs.

Poem Placed in an Old Pair of New Balance Sneakers and Left on New Balance Factory Outlet Store Stoop on Berrigan's Birthday November 15 2016

my name is
[your name]
and I am your constituent –
not even the angels
want to wear my red shoes
from the overflowing brim

a high-mind american
moral bargain bin
walked too far with
worn down heals,
the ghosts of old balance –
power, its stultifying molds

the dream of keeping it together, –
tender not fragile – being
"the literary one" at the office,
asked to explain difference
between Roman and Greek Tragedy
while a childhood speaks its riot

fear, taken out of context,
fails both sides of the divide
this one being neither
violet thrush or sunburst sits
until the end of the anthem,
stands before the game already begun

Poem to be Read Aloud on the Corner of Massachusetts Ave. and Newbury St. on International Worker's Day

I'm there with the strobers,
for the thieves. I can read
heavy arrivals and
smile anyway; why not?
tagging bottomless cotton
blends until this shift ends
too early for stars
I pass k.d. lang
one morning, eyes locked in
that say don't. So I didn't.
Too tired to give.

Barefoot hippies take the square the day Jerry Garcia died,
drum circles bleat crosstown tie-dyed poly-rhythms,
waiting on Mister-Mountain-Dew-Baggy-Pants to replace me
on the late shift. I'm there on time.

When the old lady farts
for the morning meetings
we pretend not to
proof the memo the day she dies.

I'm there for the changing room loose needles thousand-dollar wallets for the kind homeless man asking for King James
for mortar-boards textbook returns crossed bridges to soft
Pluto, for empty karma stolen out from tarot decks.

I'm there when the lady
touched my forehead for the pulse of an aura
another pukes Scope & both colors change.
I'm there when the Patriots lose to the Giants.

I'm there when the Patriots lose to the Giants.
I'm there to follow
so many woke dreamers to the mattresses.
Am I there? For the feel
fitting in after all this time
can I help ? can I help ? can I
deny myself the question

step from behind the register, the back of my hand
a makeshift blind against winter slant after
noon sunset: commerce – an open mouth
emptying its ringing song on corners
for the work that wants the wheel
that wants the drum to shake it all loose from

Poem for The Earth Archive
for Danielle Vogel

This ash is from
A poem I burned
But had intended on sending
In the dream I wear purple
Ribbons on my shoulder
I was a winner I was
MR MASSACHUSETTS
but wrong to think this
song is about me. Forgive me
I had misread your instructions as
"This sash is from"
your purple halo burnt against the sky

•

This air is from
an empty purse of island
print, imperfect &
lonely, as dull things –
monied – go
unbroken, through space
passed through,
& through the between
celebrants chant
U ! S ! A ! US! A!
& you reply:
UP! ALL NIGHT!
UP ! ALL ! NIGHT !

•

This water's from
a yak's beard
that drinks its lake reflection
in a Tibetan portrait exhibit.
Or at least, it wished it was:
this water's really
from the bubbler
that missed your mouth,
daubed the sneaker
you wore last time to this museum
to see some other portrait.
Yes, you have a membership.
It says you are a frequent visitor.

•

This earth is from
the dirt dug for the planet
flung up to the stratosphere
hovers among tomorrow's
islands (sorry
for the clutter)
with this groovy digger's song.
It's Saturday morning in the Universe
& around the earth, people
look wonderful together.

Poem for Empire

There's a lot in (the history of the United States) ... that you're proud of, and then there's a lot of things in it that you're ashamed of. And that burden, that burden of shame, falls down. Falls down on everybody. – Bruce Springsteen on The River Tour, 1981

To Fall,
falling
(accidental) from accident
building to aircraft –
burning animal (in sport
private or transport)
animal-drawn vehicle
Falling down balcony
escalator bed
ladder bicycle
in boat, ship, bridge
watercraft building
staircase burning
stairs, steps – private
see Fall, from, cable car
stairs, earth (not on rails)
(with asphyxia chair
or suffocation cliff
(by pressure)) curb (sidewalk)
see also elevation aboard ship
Earth, due to accident
falling embankment
escalator

Falling from, off
aircraft flagpole
(at landing) gangplank
(in-transit) (into water)
(while alighting, (see also Fall, from)
boarding) to deck, dock
resulting hammock on ship

haystack
high place
stated as undetermined whether accidental or intentional —
see Jumping, from, horse
ladder
machinery
pedal cycle
playground
railway rolling stock, train, vehicle (while alighting, boarding)

Falling, with
collision
derailment
explosion
rigging (aboard ship)
scaffolding
structure
burning
toilet

tower
tree
turret
viaduct
wall
wheelchair
window

Falling in, on
aircraft
watercraft
cutting or piercing instrument or machine —
see Cut
glass, broken
knife
see cut, object, edged, pointed or sharp —
see Cut

Falling into
cavity
dock
hold
hole
manhole
moving part of machinery —
see accident, machine
opening in surface
pit
quarry
shaft
storm drain
tank

water	
well	
late effect of	
	Falling
Falling,	through
over	
animal	
cliff	due to
embankment	accident
small object	due to
overboard	watercraft
rock	roof
as avalanche	window
stone	timber
	railway train
	street car
	empire
	waterfall

Poem for a Disappearing Roommate
for Nathan Child

The mad old monk has abandoned
Your star that looks like a poker game
One prong on its lock turns white –
Lone rock on the lawn boo forever.
You're so beautiful it's starting to rain
in the Appalachians, we plant a champion
living tomb, in the soon green ground –
The sum, for mouths, of these wishes.

You don't need to see anything out
to seek anything out of the ordinary:
today is not an attempt at misrepresentation –
anchors must still be built with skill;
nobody just doing things where they're going
who knows they're not where they are,

Mountains belong to people who love them;
that you've succeeded in putting them there.
Should I call today loneliness, lucidity or
black roses for a blue lady fancy pants?
The word I forgot just now – yes.
Here's to embarrassment even lonelier than snow
knocked back to the zipper of the shadows.

If you try fighting magic with logic
a beautiful thing spreads beauty all around;
if you risk facing your captors alone
a friend comes over to the house;
if you think a page's the disguise
oceans beyond us the distance you imagine;
if you decide it's too risky, turn

from the bridge which is seldom free:
leaves, all the dirt in the furrows,
the river of song: seek them for
the question. Still with some unforeseeable
break in the frost of the last chrysanthemum
for its own sake, for going on
a suit put down to the ground.
A favor for which to be forever.

Poem for Alice Coltrane On International Women's Day

"Help but consider the manifold forces of desire"

Half a leaf is night...
Black fig,
Beet-water
Succulents,
Lavender,
Balsam oil,
Ylang ylang.
Marijuana strawberry
Mushroom + pepperoni
Willow bark
Rosemary mint
Chamomile.

...the other half is Sister Turiyasangitananda arising from repose on a couch in the mirror gold room   lords and mantras pass through her fingers as celestial music tips the three gates open...

Organ and harp,
Drums and wind chimes.
The Ankh of Amen-Ra.

Sycamore Flesh

To Be Read Aloud & Placed on a Sycamore Trunk Outside JFK's Birthplace 84 Beals Street Brookline MA Independence Day 2018

    1

Burn cedar sandalwood
    piñon for this question

      isn't *are* you suffering
   but who you're suffering *with*
   a lack that shocks itself awake
              from blunt-armed tragedy
                 the repertoire
              pretty evenly split
                along fascist lines

              Order me another
              no thank you,
              with courage to outrage,
                out-edge age

  one-thousand paper cranes
     your arms are dreams to heal in

  I'd be okay a hummingbird
     in mist upstaged by blooms

    2

child brandishes
  a head-sized snowball
    through crowded crosswalks

    tossing & catching
        tossing & catching
            & catching

    doesn't make a map for any meeting
        under the orphan ceiling's
            geography of loss

    3

like how to cope with this shit's with this know how
that can will or does not wash itself ashore
a shape less like rain than thunder
less like a mob than moth-brim
less like a walk-the-plank than pliant page of cups
more like a damned saint in oracle fever
more like what summer stalks sing back in bulk,
hungry knots that leak thirst,
how what empties from a borderless world will remember you

Philip Whalen Sitting Zazen

— Amida, Buddha of
Infinite Light
blind drawing @ MFA 18/1/15

Sunshine Umbrella

We're in a band called Sunshine Umbrella write our symphony by chance assembly of ants wandered across blank music pages lured with a dummy picnic basket of sauces and vinegar loathed by critics hailed by Occupations of Loneliness you will shred on uke be the soundtrack to teenage petting travel upper Mongolia open an eponymous coffee shop be forgotten and remembered have lovers and misadventures survive pinkeye and the van fire come back as ants and meet then in a swimming pool of an inverted umbrella tossed away from the picnic after summer rain so hello again banana hello HELLO from this umbrella in the sun loops of our own music we've been singing this whole time...

My Heart Is Full of Buffalo Wings
for Joe Cooper

Because my love is a personal broken record for the most wild crispy mediums eaten in one sitting, my heart is full of buffalo wings and greasy pre-residues. When we come back in the bar from smoking a stranger's thumbing the book you left behind. Everyone seems the same kind of nervous, but you're not. He talks crazy wisdom, *sometimes I wonder…* Months later in the blink you'll send I still can't read the monk but hear what he's laughing: *sometimes I wonder if I am a butterfly dreaming that I am a man or if I am a man dreaming I am a butterfly.* Sometimes from the inside-out I wonder what a heart attack might look like, maybe a monk laughing at the moon all round while all around randomness sings all around Mama There Goes That Man, Rudies All Around, The Love You Save (May Be Your Own). Above the dark bar are Dodgers and Giants. When you see me in the mirror I forget which one I am…

Love Parade

What's with that row of black cars snaking from your dried-lilac-behind-the-ears distraction drama, a lonely lunch in the rational park? One moment bright enough to fill the half-frame with a hawk on chain/link, the next a sleazy midnight retrospective of the Empire State's grittier days: each moral foyer's lit a-flicker with little drunken siren jokes, glittery day-for-nights to jump the hitch off your shadow. The feels you're outside of or at home within con/stella ruins coupled with ivory char sketches of Tuileries dresses and hi-hat revelers. Cut to: a daughter explains G-Chat as rupture in the disco scene: "My sainted aunt! Sainted Donna Summer, I remember yesterday's revelry beveraged under…" infamously flushed in a synth laden gold room with disintegrating lusters, glitch-ridden electrostatic tweety mumbles. I feel a last dance coming on: conga line in mourning filling up emptiness, a stop bath peopled in unfinished neon, faces hungry without recourse. The heart-as-usual grid and groove was on the up, but the feel was off. Thus we turn to the streets in these times of treble. We tune these streets.

Auld Lang Signifier

You are chosen to play a traditional song at the National Tree Lighting Ceremony. Initial confidence soon turns to dread when you remember you haven't played the song in a long while, cannot remember the melody, and are not, in fact, a pianist. Desperate pleas to spare yourself from public humiliation go unheard by the kindly but insistent lady organizers, and you cannot procure sheet music, or a spare practice piano. No, no choice but to go along with understandable reserve, take your seat at the instrument as festive, patriotic crowds gather by the oval, the national orchestra and dueling orphan choruses are placed at the candied stage banks, and the cameras begin their slow, calculating zooms. Only later, awake in bed, will you realize that the score had been in the piano bench on which you sat, and due to sensitivities of aging instruments and their players to the season's cold, the ensemble – yourself included – had pantomimed to a pre-recorded soundtrack all along. For auld lang syne.

Poem for Businessmen or, Wrong Shirt

Before a big production meeting some businessmen, interviewees and clients alike, gather in the public restroom, primping and adjusting, rehearsing phrases in the mirror like so many hot-air hand-dryers... when some invisible Pan removes their shirts and flings them in a cottony mountain on the restroom floor. Now each stripped of their carefully shaped professional identity, the men desperately sift the pile for their own kind of blue. The relative similarities in the cuts, sizes, and colors result in discombobulating false starts, discomfits from an unfamiliar pattern, an errant collar, a purple stain or wild cuff. Despite frantic obfuscations, the men collectively pull together, but by the time of the meeting, any attempts to impress or intimidate with hard-line tactic proves ineffective, as each man from the bathroom looks around the table: slight, out-of-breath, discolored faces, silent and fearing that at some critical line item negotiation, they may be exposed by a savvier, more opportunistic businessman, who might break their silent pact... though, troubling the line, if one were to be exposed, the whole outfit would be implicated... that each and every one at that table was wearing the wrong shirt.

The Great Midwestern Hardware Store
i.m. Prince

What's love's thunder but to rattle? What fates await The Great Midwestern Hardware Store? They are so good at normal space, folding front pages of the senses into foxed thistles in pasted on shadows over second-hand whispers, damp zinnia beneath the awninged sun. You can't take a microchip to coffee, better to bounce some ideas off a thoughtful human brain intuiting recoup benefits of later second plantings. Anselm always seems to know the score – oh, he can read the moon a-waxin'. Wowee zowee, says Mr. McGee, at Burt's new trowel, replacing one slipped forgetfully into mossy loam last late fall before the first frost. Cranking up his Walkman, a young Prince freaks on Zappa, lids closed, humming bridges of a slow & lonely panic, riding out the bells with a quiet night in, returning to the cosmic egg among haunted stars. In his suit of clouds, inspired by the door, through the door he goes: to cross the most jaywalked city street on earth called Joy Street. The dust-like money settles, no extra for the tumbling. Blown headphones left behind, swaying on the rakes.

Begging Bowl

The International space station: brighter today than Venus (the goddess) planets that wave back on astronauts who remember the whale mama nudges her dead calf, backwards & around flowing through both, rivering the source. On air an activist says, *when we say people, we mean skeletons*. Grief, sadness, outrage. Winners, losers. Old robe, new person: current flowing backwards & around the first to sing to half-a-million expectant people of your generation gathered in a muddy field when your repertoire's done but you need to keep singing because the next act's not ready yet so you just sing whatever like *sometimes I feel like a motherless child*, sweating the strap sticks to your dashiki while guitar strings snap & glisten. When we sweat through the pores of our backs, we glisten. We make the shape of the song ringing back the shape: the shape of a begging bowl.

Philip Whalen sitting zazen.
Philip Whalen sitting zazen.
Philip Whalen sitting zazen.
Philip Whalen sitting zazen
Philip Whalen sitting zazen.
Philip Whalen sitting zazen.
Philip Whalen sitting zazen.
Philip Whalen sitting zazen.
Mauve couch.

Brighton Night

BRIGHTON NIGHT
for Diane DiPrima

my mother is a screaming beatles girl
aunt gail's for the rougher stones
cedar   eucalyptus
         soy   wax   amber
sage
& cold toned clovers
crimson
& still I go   still getting down
to the thirties over-
night   better throw another blanket on
thin
city tree keeps hinting at a renaissance
sunflower   rosemary   beeswax to my lips

BEING LISTING

alights
against the world
and not above it

OVER

and to think
I thought it
somewhat

HOKUSAI

have you seen the great wave?
one hundred bridges in a single view

THE ART OF TOWING PART 2

Goodbye Hummer
Your joke was the color of my bummer

SOON

drone plane
fly above it

WALKING ACROSS WHOLE FOODS PARKING LOT

high inside the mind granola

THERE ARE THOSE

of us through
and <u>through</u>

LANDING

in spite of
or actually
in spite of

PERCEPTION

door left open which invites
participation in quite enough

RERUN

peace, please
syndicate
every summer

OPPOSITE BILLIONAIRES

do they still owe
us
one scorpion

AND BACK

to the rotunda
and back

UN

Certai

Hello "world"   World.   = realistic fiction
= what we mean   when   we say what we mean

increasingly without lacking forward progress

one thousand paper cranes
for Sadako Sasaki

your arms are dreams to heal in

EXHIBEE DÉCOR

Goya gray
plums
commerce

THAT

's the truth of that?

CROMMELYNCK GATE

rainbow wrenches bunch the gates
what cannot be broken opens

ANOTHER

between trills there airs over almost gone

motor after motor
<u>another</u>

SUMMER HOURS

often offer tours even later after

APPROACH

means distance
miles & miles & miles
& <u>then</u> what?

FOUND

again
that without
knowing

LANDING

bask   y   yacht

TIM

all ways a poet,
never abide

VIRTUAL

Equivalent
Turbulent
Final third

PLAN

when it's time
it makes me

HAPPENING

behind something went

rain

rain on

rain on river

over

veery apt pupil

HOW AT

The Independent: delicate & informal
The Green Room: brash & ineloquent

what's better

threaded through mist

AIR

conditions too askew

TOPICAL MYTHOLOGY

w o l f b u b b l e s b o r n u n d e r b u n c h e s

put the cavern in the chapter on fear and stood up

huh

IS IT

I don't think it
over & over & over
eventually

BICYCLE

midtown
past the dinosaurs

b i r d l u n g
e

MOON

has a carved move left

WOODED

asking a bucket

what I went for let out

LIKE

like country gnomes I like
like the confesses of grace

TWO OF HEARTS

Heart
Beats up
In mornings

low wool low
wool low wool
low wool low
wool low wool

ANOTHER LIKE

I like how how
to cope with this
shit's with this
know-how

rot tumble bird carcass deer trembles in Alex's compost

LIBRARY

won't open
I'll go any way

CHRONOLOGY

remembrance yard
street chestnut

MOVES

<u>to</u> the edge
<u>from</u> the edge
<u>m o v e s</u> the edge

UNKNOWN VOICEMAIL

v o i c e t h e v o i c e y o u v o i c e

SOMBER EROS

Monsieur

Monsieur

Monsieur

Monsieur

you forgot

your hat

is-was-ly-has-ly
Did it

K

"between one way
or the other,
I take the other"

The inflated surround was a wonder. Ideal minimal
barrier. A product of desperation, it couldn't have
been invented better. It was pure vulnerability—
you could fall over it or cut through it easy as pie.
We were contained by will and barely anything
else.

THAT

was a wound
wasn't even known
& THAT, friends,
was how he was found
in the middle of the bossa nova

BRINK

at its best
when
it's done
gone on

PRETTY SURE

there's more than one way

APPARENTLY

w i d e e y e d a t f i v e

NO JOKE

should it be
about that cold
being more than
only you can
take be only one

PEOPLE

look wonderful together

in from the sound
ring for the bell

April
showers
bring
May

impeachment hearings

BIDE

kiss
good
night
its
morning

Three adults,
Two strollers,
A dog. A fish
Eye floating

EPIPHANY, OR

optic ebb
comforts
foaming
in the glut

where u belong i belong

*Nine square inches of divine turmoil.
Rotating on its spinner or cooking on
its stand, the Kalliroscope models the
action on the surface of the Earth and
in all the waves and fires and
(probably) in your head.   —SB*

(pretty much everything you can imagine)
LIFTING   UP

F O U R S T A R S I N A A → R O W ★★★★

Two pink sails go any which way
fortunately bluely unambiguously

DEATH ROW RECORDS
Sobbing on bus bench

WRINKLES

from back his friends' hands'
smoother
there's a ring around the moon

MORE barn
WHAT owl?

RASPBERRY

never did find what
i was looking for - -
they say it's good luck

SOLSTICE

'trying' to think of nothing

neither over nor out - -

Where are all the Druids?

totter along edge of vibrant
downslope - -

"Its overpriced,
but I didn't have to pay"

ANSELM

another summer
love, Jane
no end
in sight - -
ho ho !

THE MUMPS!

plums
jingle in
my helmet

Can you
know
Every way
H E R E

shell
& old shingle

ACTUAL
Trunkful of
flan

there's everything and then there's everything and whatever's left

now and then i row and row lonely as an oar
under that one big star

BOTH BOTH

Gold & white and
Blue & black
AND blank stars
on crush impulse

Dreamt
singing in traffic
& how to dance
The Avalanche

A rest
THE will
milky rays
nourishment

clear wax bulb pops off the cap
blisters in a crowd of painters

NEON GULL
aight aight aight

PROBLEMS

not yours to keep
'all i got's done
gone'

Emotionally

Playful

Oboes

NICELY SLEEPING
Water giant
scatters moths
in sharp delay
from the dull full ridge

<u>Daniel Webster Estuary</u>

excessive damage
looms
clever as
a goose
water sirens

SLOW ROLLER

drags its meat
past the heater,
half the vinyl

siding still to set,
the son to drive
home,
radio between them.

door swings open on its simple hinge
bags packed with I'm not ready to go

GET LOST

looking how far back
i may have left to go,

SHALLOW
MELLOW

a distance
a following away
a flowing out
a decoy

raven punching me in the face don't stop now

VIDEO VOICE

Where is your horror?
We don't have a horror.
I'm looking for Dead Man.
They're all checked out.

OVER

the   the   the
borderline   representation

late July late !

IRENE DUNNE

plays it cleverly
tipsy   convincing
Cary Grant
being Cary Grant
all it's cracked up to be

I just think
I don't know

CITY VINES

rise high as the highrises rise
higher even

C A A A R L O O O S

SOON

drone plane
flew above it

K

"only their wise donkey, plodding
sensibly behind, is oblivious"

HIGH INSIDE THE MIND GRANOLA
walking across whole foods parking lot

ROLEY

Stump
Shadow
Rotting log
Birch clump

Bobs voice
Lull o'
Western twang

OH SAY

bangled spanner can i

'02
uh oh
odd urge
to Hootie
oughtn't
aught to

UN
righteous
dignation

TALK

where you're
not sure
you end

hard to find something that isn't everywhere

LISTEN

be a little
at the threshold

TORSO OF VENUS

"It's <u>supposed</u> to be headless, darling."

TREE MUSIC

almost touching,
touching,
not touching,
almost touching again

deep smear
willow lips
blinks &
cooling hours

OVER

and to think
I thought it
somewhat

HOME

if you're not going
to

Good game.
Good game.
Good game.
Good game.
Good game.
Good game.
Good game.
Good game.
Good game.
Good game.
Good game.
Good game.
Good game.
Good game.

Desire Line

Desire Line
for Michele Lubowsky

decommissioned planes
dream a chirping blue
dream jays fill their dream bellies
read inflight raga dream zines
sip expired dream juice from
brittle-lip plastic dream yups
as dream pirate stations
antennae out dream wings
dream a dreamy silvery blue
glints across a dream ocean
submerged dreams seen from above
narrow edging dream bands
and ships and flashing signals
by flag and by funnel

        "the way is off my ship"
        "you may feel your way past"
        "i require a pilot"

glide thru slow desire paths
replacing dream with cloud
corrigenda with hull color
dream black dream red
dream silver or aluminum
letter G by a color signifying
gold no sea above, no air below
will dust to dust my dream must,
my desire lines clouding
every eyeline a boneyard in the air
the machine mistakes as vineyard
and so, a vineyard

Blue Acrobat
i.m. Bobbie Louise Hawkins

        i make my living in the air,
smuggled by steam, by dragonfly,
by any note or letter
                sung to hold such grief,
                        could call itself
      the flogging   anthem never stood for.

  What's left are these excuses.
Alarms. Humidity. The sirens
                having made a hole a hold from a sum.
          Maybe you are not who you are,
              this music in my jaw
            kisses, and as it kisses, leaks
                  smooth jazz at the bank.
                          No 's' on plural,
    no hiss at the end of poor.

                Blues'n greens're.
          Normal sensing   normal fill
      wades the current inlet
off the coast god summers   shrooming
  round the bend to a hoist,

the pitch of what takes when shimmers gawk, &
        rooming that glint without a net, what's left's
                lemon essence, my summer mixes
        mixing into yours

hands still wringing out the winter
                  sound of that old door opening the woods
& all you pass through, respooling rung

rings a handheld bell fixed with garlands & quiet

 is it over? i don't think it's over
    & over & over & over it
goes, when i think of nothing
      & i'm so done with nothing
 turning a way from the sea

High Contrast
after Gabor Szabo

Breezin'

wind as slight a yellow
butterfly   above her
                shorter
 "we alter things
       we haven't made ourselves"

•

Amazon

 "can you stop suffering
       for, like, a minute?"
the consensus is
an engine is dumber than a gun
& that's hard.
What's "move forward"?
Anything can
call an apse an apse.
What's that BOOMING out there?
What's "an economy"?
Grease the rose of reason?

•

Fingers

Of an out-of-range-
quaker sculpting
color on the sites
of former theatres
to project

all forgotten loves
on the scrim of
your closed eyes.
Hold on
to what you have –
so little. Of.

•

Azure Blue

If a flag to fault
for-
giving Saints
the choice
to stand for
for, or not

"attention now
wistfully drifting
into distance"   (Sotere Torregian)

•

Just a Little Communication

from out the blue
brah yell
(passenger side)
FREE RIDE !
FREE RIDE !!
to bus stop queue
Not. Sure. Do you
think he means
his privilege
like a tooth

glistening mistily
whistles
as it loosens, falling
from the top of the order

•

If You Don't Want My Love

while bootlegging
The World Series
search results

"how do you say
'how do you say'
in French"

returns: translated
slang for French Kissing
as "to roll a shovel"

comment dites-vous
"racist Indians cap" ?

Final Score:
Bad Guys 1,
Good Guys
aren't keeping score

•

I Remember When

This place used to be
A City Sports,
A Strawberries,

The Globe Corner,
Hilltop.

There, no longer
Here, & ever
More, the body
Passes by. Queens

The mind with
Laurel.
Witch Hazel.
Money Tree.

Pink & green &
How to dance
An avalanche.
Peace Lily.

Some Pleasant Moments in the 21st Century
i.m. Bill Corbett

Outside a city target

The water in the bottle left behind wobbles
Boggling the mind across the aisle
The fate of an ocean
Notices water in the bottle left behind
Wobbles watering the mind across its bauble
Bubbling without treble
The trouble with the fate of water
In the bottle left behind
Bobbing as the train curls
Logging in the mind's eye's
IRLs across URLs
The isle's not a trouble but the base
Continues long past its broad failed aim
Resembles a traveling abandon

•

K-L-E-E-N ME

Dust written
passenger side of
democracy
with absent
pointer finger.
I may be asleep
at the switch
but I dream
in spellcheck,
motherfuckers.

•

Don't puke on my heart
& tell me it's lavender –
it's that kind of a like.
A held out naming,
a blissed out missing,
the love I wish
I didn't miss
      within it.
The auditorium labeled
A U D I T O R I U M S.
Stage hands scramble the blackout
under the hull of a crazy boat
named
That One Happy Joy Division Song.

•

That One Happy Joy Division Song

Follows itself
& all I'm left for's remembering
What's flatter than the moon to sail under:
please use common sense
When you walk the streets with all that's left:
Sister, visit!
Redundancy, teach!
When I wish for you machines surround,
can't keep up in time.
Tylenol & trash bags
Crossed off the same list.

•

My conservative colleague

& I we peer at fresh strawberry bundles picked from inner city school gardens over corporate twitter feed, a brief indulgence on the thin company dime. Outside: cracking ice, distant shelves, an economy undone by the weight of sighs. Conditioned air turns down the bridge, & I pick out insipid little showstoppers: "Well, *you* know where the gardens are." I still have to do the work.

•

On the Moonlanding Anniversary or,
Summer in the City by The Lovin' Spoonful

Learned just about everything I think
I can handle from you right now,
Lavender cherry blueberry mandarin ghosts –
Baseless pinnacles proportional to collapse –
The directions pulling in every way abound,

Eclipse-eager.
Guess it's time to learn another question,
Guess it's time to teach me one more thing:
You better bring it with you when you roll though,
The learner doesn't get to set the lesson.

•

Net Neutrality

Brash, unrefined upcycled ash
built around tension-heated prairies

in bold dislocation:
an outer space waterfall
named Velvet Demon –

"even sharks suffer broken hearts"
even more than life attacks —

from miles and miles away,
my weightless
weightless cat-clicks.

•

Jupiter or Suspiria?

searching for an atm on the way to meet you at some cash only bar
downtown surrounded by unfathomable realms, stupefying wealths

the last voice of high rises walking it back, talking
moccasin attached to the bottom of a crutch

walking it back, regretful. leaning.

•

The 1987 NBA Finals Video

A sky's more than hook shot
Shots and shots of shot bulk
pink fragrant dogwood buds

Crossed fingers, fingered
crosses ring the bell, even on detour
etch a plaid and hoop love on a coffin ride

Replay when stuck between
Stops and crossed stops
boinging against bank brick

So, it's all come to this...—
Lew Welch or Lew Alcindor

Gone 'til November

What you feel is not a draught but a breeze
They led me away
The linen didn't stir

Not at home to arrive
What if I still don't know
How to touch

And still believe I'm human
(Perhaps no one will notice
Being nestled where we are)

Greet this slow and siren
Put these flowers in a vase and
let's get on with things

Ask more questions
Luging thru the air singing
This is the day / the day has made

Something to think about:
That we loved all outer space,
Resemble one another

Follow the Essay on Beginnings Until…
[Rest of Quote Unfound]

Dearly beloved, walking you home,
summer streetlamp's black moon-framed
green leaves, notice no ice, no winter, no
bunnies, only global *waming* walking you
home. Thrushes in shrubs I see bunnies in
after walking you home. Awkward dog owners
under park light socialize: "some dogs aren't
quite socialized" with waggy little doggy butts,
walking you home. Forever's pretty long so
here's a song for you, a spiral rainbow prism
for a 4 AM shiftless shuffle, sometimes for self-
preservation your thought's a loving text, for sure
as sure is, is walking me home, after walking you
home, is making me be leaf again, and grown
again, going, and whole again, our love a poem
without end, each way walking us home,
which is meant to say, oh! ha! Beginnings.
Walking you home is walking me home.
I love you more than Purple Rain

EVERYBODY IS A STAR
i.m. Marthe Reed

                                      there you go

                beyond light

                                              as you were,

WEATHER, NOT OCEAN

Even solitude dissolves
along, undulant. Tide hand
reaching heights, cool lean

against the bar. Dusk
leaving meaning, leaving
song, treeness saps

green – even where
no silence – goes and so:
returns else nearer bloom.

Tows the bunk path's
seed patch. Feathered rudders'
crisp blind curls for tracing

sharp body-bound flasks,
backyard bark dog, piss
briar: lioness sky.

Really, that this knows you.
That you know, want's,
enough. No difference

steams the crescent splay
Fence post muds the ring bath
towards out the cruel loop.

Little yellow wild clouds
still slightly, push away from
purpose, the moment's

snap back strains
stand against
precious fenestra

gold sea jetsam
a rare and mundane strand
kind, but throw down

your heat, too. Make sure
you have your say.
Aims analogous.

Bright surfaced northern bands.
A tonal lightening stray
buzz inside reclusive lumens

Touch earth, pinks gypsum
lady-slipper. Sandy hill –
the knob broad crow –

Can it be live-forever? If.
Rock-ribbed flags, coarse
rush, the passing sapling.

Cakes in a rainstorm bob
Almost Periodic Oscillations
and Waves – come not,

impatience of clouds!
desperate carry, balance
an ocean to go

either azalia – desire,
untrained keeps watch
asking even, tide,

help me turn the boat around.
"I think of you today
as one cloud less, where

there's one lone sea plane, too"
Excerpts – altitudes
to mind – large

as night's nightly
sloped beast
paths to the reef.

R.E.M. Suite

You're gonna have to start thinking your way out of this economy.
— Mark Bradford's Spiderman

Murmur

The rain I fear:
Just as wet ~
Rain I do not fear

Can't push any further
False door
Between afters
Hopped into

Heavier vessels
These modal boats
Bob in tone

Patience
Leading patience

•

Reckoning

Down a one-way mirror,
elastic energy drops
ecclesiastical junk
from Latin silver's
New Spain:

"Regardless of racial
heritage, people could

legally change their caste
by demonstrating outstanding
citizenship or paying
money to the king"

Hanging or cover?
I would like again see the river,
not the harbor it leads to

•

Fables of the Reconstruction of the Fables

This early lesson
Not a culture,
But a continent

In the naming
Am I part of the club,
The columns

Of exclusion?
Ships of ice,
Makes of sails

Not the club,
The determined to
not to say

The boundaries we are / taught
The boundaries we are / beyond
The boundaries we are not

•

Lifes Rich Pageant

Around every action
we become
The richness, its embrace
Around, along, among –

Am I doing it wrong?
Rocky coast and gulls
Around along, among

Document

Across the river is
Across the street
A good way of getting there

Only you know
Where you're going
Bottled at the moment
Among the maulers

Though we're rose,
An offering
Are pastry all day
Without jogging

Taut kinks ~
Surface of rain
Joining deeper surfaces

Dear Reed Bye,

during prolonged creative dormancies
I reassembles as the unwatered, wilting
houseplant, thirsty stems pressed to winter
glass, cool to the feather, sharing room
with an empty pot of once boiled water for-
gotten, gas flame still burrowing below, runty
air kicks back a click of tin fizzle, no hand near,
the dry knowledge of soil slips back to second
in line for a need   should there be attendance –
there should be attendance – as patience
in becoming, stress the sampling weighs,
indestructible molecules fire gently
as tomb glow flicker against alien mummy wrap
touching down its trample, a kind of tingle in
the ankle, transfer balking as its root,
a booster if there will be

An autumnal

falls full husk back
how long the search
for what's not
lost, if to love's
an ease of, being
close enough, say
no – sweetly – to
and not have it
hurt like that
ambrosic cabaret
moth cobalt bowl
with a planet planted in
when the deal goes down it goes as most deals do: through oblivion
      enough to steep tall grasses & keeps in / cracks around the ring
from that one bad year while we hold out our tongues for a last flake in
           the heat. is this how to leave one with everything
                        quiet wading waiting
        against river light
      against a shadow's
      single branch –
        fells
       lowed
        opens –
              & love these words into smoke

WATER LILIES
after Monet

Caution is the moth
        you move on in a blip
                a perilously reductive glint

unspooling, half-thought
        around all you pass through
                to get at what you know.

An arrow drives the wheel-
        reflective sky, shows Pedernal
                through the eye holes.

Sturdy is the burning
        temple – when the temple
                was a bubble to blink at,

a shored up density flow.
        Ye chemical Aztec,
                walk on by! across the sky!

sextiles & trines
        droplets puddle, shimmer
                the letter-ringed pharaoh's

moondog karma.
        A muzzle of light
                lifts off a tired old

riff, blinks green
        as violet stone
                before the rip spools

Other Delights

Morning's rider blunders,
turns in wonder over rivers
Underwater, a thirsty thirsty
Ardor, kinda bursting
A clear *refelction*
Wiped clean with
The back of my face
Makes it rougher,
Belly scratch with
Crescent amethyst
Where the moon once was
My device corrects
(Wrongly) as amateur
Amateur painters
Amateur poets
Amateur loners
Auteur lovers,
other heroes we're over
The river steams of any code
Opens yup that door
Let the strollers pass
Let me on my way
Be my way
In leather thistle
Burns the skull
Through & tussle,
Rough as soft is
Morning's rider
Fawning over blunders,
Other delights

Elegy with Saffron & Honey
i.m. David Berman

afraid sometimes
to die i sleep alone
in the big big city
in the big big big big
night   off leash
from chariots of flesh

speaking of wham
& colonial pulldowns

designed to lie among stars that live
their endless displays
drain the beautiful from beauty,
a weak yet faithful flash
coils in their drawl
around an unfinished front
inside naval reach,
a retrograde ignored.

Take this golden palm,
give me license & chariot
sting a song & sing a sign
another star
vaguely errant

wanders from blunderings
loosed from the spangled order
as bling at the tiki-bar
galactic ancient tenements

laughing in rhythm
laughing on key
laughing back at the laughers
air spilling everywhere

"the red-gold turning gray"
could you imagine
dancing in the aisles
stomping in time
the tune of this sweet slinging sphere

Two Sherpas

Goodnight Cassiopeia
I love you your helm is showing
softly as a navigator on fire
of fire generous to new life
as bees in gallant weather

A purple halo burnt against the sky,
stolen gems jostle in a velvet bag
blue plums brushed by a siren's flask
ambrosia sips from a begging bowl

With a desire to paint water
on our warm math of honeymoons
the jasmine continues to steep past being done
melting the sparks of our fur

We follow each other up
two Sherpas, tum-
blinging forwards
your helm is showing

Goodnight, Cassiopia
symphony! symphony!

The Beginning
i.m. Joanne Kyger

The Beginning is for what i always want to be
(no beginnings, and without reservation)
where it seems you've always been.

Tonight might not snow on the poor
whippoorwill singing just delineations
of emotion through bleak measure's fair

night outside the repertory of bad science
fiction, my loneliest guilty pleasure.
How fear keep us in wonder

apropos democracy,
cf. "do we really care
about the magna carta?"

or the always dream of being
one of a billion breathing comets crashing
around the tropic scientific expedition,

we few'd be select not for expertise
but for kindness & ability to learn & teach
knowing the best "learn bring rest to others."

Chef, singer, poet-astronomer, fire-swallower,
a hip old scientist like Kyger in a lab coat
leads us daily to our study: soil effects on

turtle migration, kelp flow on otter populations,
sand in the eye on dispersals of methods.
Slowly, what we learn from everybody: play

ukulele in unique ways – i mean modern ukulele –
identify each star song & bird flights solstice
gifts us from this, our daily pain,

take what we have from what we can, continue
giving away, return to one another's friends
i to yours, you to mine, – if you so choose –

take me to where you belong.
Readjust to this new life of infinite
divisions, love's indivisibles. Learn

from what we can, leave the rest behind
in the greened-out seventies-before-
the-giant squid-attacks-me-kind-of-fear,

with no locks, just respect for cucumbers
we call friends, find some ways for fuller living
inside the ← all ↓ ways ↑ dream →
where we do the daily waking

After a 2006 dream where Allen Ginsberg invites me to pick his set-list for a poetry reading in a medieval village barn. I choose a leather-bound volume called The Beginning. *Awake, I discover Allen does not have a poem called* The Beginning.

Notes.

The epigraph is taken from the following by Anni Albers, as it appeared in *Black Mountain College Bulletin* in 1941: "The difficult problems are the fundamental problems; simplicity stands at the end, not at the beginning of a work. If education can lead us to elementary seeing, away from too much and too complex information, to the quietness of vision, and discipline in forming, it again may prepare us for the task ahead, working for today and tomorrow." Quoted in *Black Mountain Poems: An Anthology*, edited by Jonathan C. Creasy (New Directions, 2019).

Arsonist's Daughter – Title is the name of the character Grady Tripp's acclaimed novel in Michael Chabon's acclaimed novel *Wonder Boys*. "Flames on the side of my face. Heaving, breathless heaving breaths…" is a monologue by Mrs. White played by Madeline Kahn in the 1985 ensemble comedy *Clue*.

Cluster Glitters – "you know, he said, you have a real talent for dreams / I had hoped, of course that the world would stand still" are lines from correspondence between Ann Charters and Charles Olson, from *Evidence of What is Said* (Tavern Books).

Call Script – "No one's in charge, the situation's the boss." Attributed to tour roadie Steve Parish in *Long Strange Trip*, a documentary about The Grateful Dead, directed by Amir Bar-Lev.

Poem for Nasty Women – I can't find the direct source of the quotations "simplicity defies resolution" and "step out of your comforts of illusion". Their Buddhist wisdom and approximate timing might point toward hearing pianist Herbie Hancock's Norton Lectures at Harvard University.

Fenway Park Poem – Flower names were notated in a used copy of the popular field guide *How to Know the Wildflowers*, by "Mrs. William Starr Dana", whose real name was Frances Theodora Parsons (Scribner's, 1911). The book's previous owner wrote detailed notations of her flower observations throughout New England over a period of 50 years, beginning in the 1910s.

New Balance Poem – A week following the 2016 Election, athletic apparel New Balance's VP of Communications Matt LeBretton made a pro-Trump comment in regards to the then-president-elect's position on the Trans-Pacific Partnership. Social media response to the company included product bans, and social media influenced shoe destruction.

Poem for The Earth Archive – Poet Danielle Vogel commissioned this poem to appear in The Earth Archive at RISD Museum, Providence RI. The exhibit welcomed visitors to "engage with the elemental principles of art and nature through chance encounters, musical reverie, poetic musings, and art explorations—all incorporating elemental themes of fire, water, air, and earth."

Poem for Empire – Found poem from the International Classification of Diseases Clinical Modifications (ICD-9-CM) Professional Edition for Physicians.

Poem for a Disappearing Roommate – Cento collages lines from books left behind by an oft-travelling roommate. The poem's form – stanza length, line word count, quotation length, and page location of source material – was determined by chance methodology (I-Ching consultation).

Poem for Alice Coltrane – "help but consider the manifold forces of desire": from Alice Coltrane's liner notes to her spiritual jazz masterpiece *Universal Consciousness* (Impulse Records, 1971).

Brighton Night – "The inflated surround was a wonder…" and "Nine square inches of divine turmoil" squares are taken from somewhere within the pages of *The Next Whole Earth Catalog*, a rascally collection on DIY, self-sufficiency, ecology and alternative education edited by Stewart Brand.

Desire Line – A desire line (or desire path) is an unplanned path, usually worn from use over time by common passage. The quoted phrases in the middle of the poem are taken from Single Flag Meanings in International Code Flags. Appears in *Flags, Funnels & Hull Colors* by Colin Stewart; Revised Edition by John Styring (Adlard Coles Ltd.).

Gone 'til November – Title is taken from a Wyclef John song on his album The Carnival. Poem is a cento collages and adapts last lines on page 30 of books by Barbara Guest, S. Whitney Holmes, Nicole Brossard, Diane Di Prima, Lisa Ciccarello, Dorothea Lasky, Joanne Kyger, Helen Adam, Lisa Jarnot, Barbara Henning, Akilah Oliver, Sappho, Susie Timmons, Hoa Nguyen, Kelin Loe, Jenelle Porter interviewing Jessica Jackson Hutchins, and Elissa Gabbert.

Follow the Essay on Beginnings Until… – cf. Mary Ruefle's seminal *Madness, Rack, and Honey: Collected Lectures* (Wave Books, 2012).

R.E.M. Suite – Titles are taken from the band R.E.M.'s five early 1980s albums released on the independent I.R.S. label prior to being signed by Warner Bros. Mark Bradford quote appeared in video installation *Darkness Made Visible* at Museum of Fine Arts, Boston in 2015. "Regardless of racial heritage…" taken from a curator's caption to a painting at MFA (painting forgotten).